The
Auroras

Also by David St. John

Hush (1976)

The Shore (1980)

No Heaven (1985)

Terraces of Rain: An Italian Sketchbook (1991)

Study for the World's Body (1994)

In the Pines: Lost Poems, 1972–1997 (1998)

The Red Leaves of Night (1999)

Prism (2002)

The Face: A Novella in Verse (2004)

LIMITED EDITIONS

For Lerida (1973)

The Olive Grove (1980)

A Folio of Lost Worlds (1981)

The Man in the Yellow Gloves (1985)

The Orange Piano (1987)

The Figure *You* (1998)

PROSE

Where the Angels Come Toward Us: Selected Essays,
Reviews and Interviews (1995)

The Auroras

New Poems

DAVID ST. JOHN

HARPER

An Imprint of HarperCollins*Publishers*
www.harpercollins.com

HarperCollins books may be purchased for educational, business, or sales promotional use. For information, please write: Special Markets Department, HarperCollins Publishers, 10 East 53rd Street, New York, NY 10022.

FIRST EDITION

Library of Congress Cataloging-in-Publication Data
St. John, David.
The auroras : new poems / David St. John.
p.   cm.
ISBN 978-0-06-208848-2
I. Title.
PS3569.A4536A95   2012
811'.54—dc22   2011021509

12 13 14 15 16 OV/QGF 10 9 8 7 6 5 4 3 2 1

for Anna Journey

Contents

The Auroras

Acknowledgments

The American Poetry Review: "My Friend Says"; "Reckless Wing."

Art Life: "The Lake."

Denver Quarterly: "Ghost Aurora"; "Aurore Parisienne"; "Père Lachaise"; "The Book"; "Dark Aurora."

Field: "Dawn Aurora"; "Lago di Como"; "Autumn Aurora"; "Florentine Aurora."

Great River Review: "The Future"; "Piñon"; "Paisley."

Kenyon Review: "Late Oracle Sonnet"; "In the Mojave"; "The Girl Who Lived in the Rain"; "The Aurora Called Destiny"; "The Swan"; "The Aurora of the Midnight Ink."

Literary Imagination: "Hungry Ghost"; "Human Fields"; "Cambria Pines"; "Creque Alley"; "The Empty Frame."

The New Yorker: "Without Mercy, the Rains Continued."

Runes: "Gypsy Davy's Flute of Rain"; "Hollywood Salvation."

The Paris Review: "Three Jade Dice."

Poetry: "In the High Country"; "From a Bridge."

Poetry International: "Pythagorean Perfume."

The Southern California Anthology: "Leaving the Valley."

The Southern Review: "The Aurora of the New Mind"; "Schopenhauer's Dog Collar"; "The Aurora of the Lost Dulcimer."

Spillway: "The Boy."

"The Aurora of the New Mind" also appeared in *The Best American Poetry 2008*, edited by David Lehman and Charles Wright (Scribner, 2008).

"Ghost Aurora" also appeared in *The Best American Poetry 2011*, edited by David Lehman and Kevin Young (Scribner, 2011).

Thanks once again to Terry Karten for her many years of support and wisdom. Thanks too to Susan Terris for her advice and suggestions.

The
Auroras

Gypsy Davy

The Lake

Opaque   the lake woke emerald

The raw decorum of the night giving way
To a slow extravagance the petal-felled touch
Of skin & mist allowed by this

First undressing of the day   So much for beauty . . .

That is   not *so much* as in
Well my friend   That's *that* nor as in I'm certain—
At last—of *something* . . . No instead I mean

What's given to us   however dulled & undeserving we remain

Is beyond our reckoning   though we gaze expectantly into the sky
Entitled to nothing & yet demanding all   like these swollen red
Poppies at the end of each sudden summer's

Rain

The Aurora of the New Mind

There had been rain throughout the province
Cypress & umbrella pines in a palsy of swirling mists
Bent against the onshore whipping winds

I had been so looking forward to your silence
What a pity it never arrived

The uniforms of arrogance had been delivered only
That morning to the new ambassador & his stable of lovers
The epaulettes alone would have made a lesser man weep

But I know my place & I know my business
& I know my own mind so it never occurred to me

To listen as you recited that litany of automatic miseries
Familiar to all victims of class warfare & loveless circumstance
By which I mean of course you & your kind

But I know my place & I know my business & baby
I know my own grieving summer mind

Still I look a lot like Scott Fitzgerald tonight with my tall
Tumbler of meander & bourbon & mint just clacking my ice
To the noise of the streetcar ratcheting up some surprise

I had been so looking forward to your silence
& what a pity it never arrived

Now those alpha waves of desire light up the horizon
Just the way my thoughts all blew wild-empty as you stood
In the doorway to leave   *in the doorway to leave*

Yet I know my place & I know my business & I know those
Melodies *melodies* & the music of my own mind

Gypsy Davy's Flute of Rain

Gypsy Davy came along
He sang so strange and sweetly

I'd filled the final page of my diary
A lovely thing given to me by The Lady of the Lake
& bound in a cover of tooled leather

The color of late-summer heather
& a single emerald spiking up at its center

To signal the green eye of the peacock carved there
So jealously guarding my words

Jealousy jealousy oh yes so much of what
I'd written in its pages only fable after fable
Of men always at odds with the truth

Men whose belief in love was so unequivocally
Selfish & provisional
The slightest little breeze off the hem of a skirt
Flowed along the river of their dreams & slowly

I learned my job was to play just a little tune

On a flute of jade & rain
To sing a simple song about the end of pain

& if you read on you'll no doubt discover those ways

Such strange tender renders new life to any
Woman or man who'd follow a song beyond the beds
Of the forgotten
                          into lavish fields of blue light

Only the luckiest lovers may claim

Three Jade Dice

The blonde carrying the tote bag full of bones
Is dressed in a chiffon blouse printed with

Persimmon-colored butterflies
& all across the desert

The sound of
Three jade dice rattling in an old man's palm—

~✦

I wish I could tell you that it's time for coffee
I wish I could tell you that the card table

Carved of onyx & ivory
Supports a life of orgasmic hope & certain prosperity

I wish I could tell you the legs of the piano reach
All the way to the ground just as

~✦

I wish I could tell you the melody of the forgotten
Is as beautiful as the melody of the desired

& I wish you'd have waited for me there beneath the sign
Of the Hotel Mallarmé or almost anywhere you claimed

You'd wait for me as those tall altars of amber dissolved
& each soft socket gathered up its lace of ash

Hollywood Salvation

Pier Paolo was polishing the crucifix out beneath the willow

He'd taken his basket of rags & set it beside the chair
& at his left side there also rested a flat porcelain basin he'd
Screwed into the sand & filled with peaches & nectarines

(There high on the Hollywood hillside the old Spanish house

Its glazed red tiles & the happiness of everything
He had imagined)   In the kitchen you could still smell the faint
Scent of cigar smoke from the night before

& in the shopping bag—the green canvas shopping bag—
The kale & avocados the cook had brought home
& like the weary brain or like the signs of a summer about to end
Or the shawl awaiting the first chill of an autumn night

He too was waiting though he didn't know why or what for

But he too was waiting & so I told him again
About visiting the relics of St. Anthony in Padova
A cool afternoon or a hot afternoon I've remembered it both ways

& one of them I know must be true I know

I walked like a sack of feathers heavy & yet fragrant with spirit
& everywhere the bones of the saint & the bones of other saints
(& of course everything I saw) were singing in the gold

Of evening every bell ringing across the shingles of the light

Every whisper of cloud every sword of psalm brightening
The soft air—so I walked quietly toward the inexplicable
To keep present the object

Of a faith so new then (I say this now to hold the memory sharp)

It became a fable of the fallen nest & the broken shell
& who now would walk beside me (I asked) into those long skies
Beyond this solitary wood to let me

Wash in that salvation flooding the day in broken light?

Pythagorean Perfume

Is that a flower in your hand Pythagoras
I thought so

Walk with me tonight underneath the universe
Its animal spirit still alive & pulsing

You know even though my vest is metal
My eyes are open

& the mystery of perfume is the perfume of mystery
Don't walk away from me now

Even in the Silver Age blaze of your song I will wake
Inside the sleeping liberties

Even if your boat is carved of rancid meat
& your sails are frozen with ice don't despair

The wind
From the south is coming

Everyone knows the changes yes even you
Who fear has crippled

The way sulphur colors the afternoon air
Even you will smell every fresh passage & the way

Between the sneering angels & the razors of the rocks

Schopenhauer's Dog Collar

It was a night of universal purpose
A night found in Schopenhauer
A kind of carved marble darkness

That flowed as fluidly as a river

It was the speculation of the coming dawn
& the twin of Schopenhauer's shadow
It was all soul devoid of reason

& just as that soul worked
Its cool magic & the day's light
Arrived like an owl sketching the shadows

With feathers of cooling ash
All along the harbor of sensual remorse
Such a prolonged white silence fell

Such a glare of weather such a design of mind
All holding themselves to the celestial wind
& beyond the black of the cemeteries

Beyond the shipwrecks & restless barking corpses
Beyond the coffins lined with an ancient purple sky
Beyond the air of the stoneless temples

& their ever-rippling echoes I knew
I would not understand the (fecund) humid green
Nor those threads of your abrupt departure

Stitching the dead into such soft blankets
As you sailed into the suspect future its jewels of moon
Shining like bared studs in Cerberus's leather collar

The Aurora of the Lost Dulcimer

My favorite Appalachian dulcimer had suddenly left "on holiday"
But that wasn't going to stop me

I went to call on the ancient blues legend in his sixth-floor
Walk-up down on The Avenues because you know

I'd come too far to let the harsh estrangement of an instrument
Collude in such a singular disappointment

I was just like Ulysses but better dressed
Against the call of all the blue sirens lighting up Desire

& the moment my riverboat had docked along the fat pier
At New Orleans I'd set off on my mission

To step right off into that long-legged darkness with nothing
To protect me but my flaming Koa 1937 Nioma Hawaiian guitar

& the faith the songs that I knew were there awaiting me
Were the lessons I could paste like armor

Along the ragged seams of my soul those soul patches
For those soul scars & finally as I knocked on his worn door

I could hear the metal clasps of his guitar case
Snapping like the jaws of an alligator biting at summer flies

Then he opened up just standing there
In a purple bathrobe over a torn T-shirt & freshly pressed jeans

Smiling the way the moon smiles down on Lake Pontchartrain
& so began my true education & the resurrection of my good name

Late Oracle Sonnet

1) Up late last night up late now this morning

2) *The new clover whitening the hillside*

3) The glass empty on the zinc counter

4) Also the white thimble of coffee awaiting you

5) *The cello she once painted turquoise & black*

6) Nobody cares nobody moves nobody thinks

7) *The spray of iris sprawled across the sofa*

8) The windows are blank with last night's rum

9) *The rhinestones suckled in the lead of the day*

10) The comfrey & the feldspar & the drying mud of night

11) *The columns made entirely of white dust*

12) That terrible taste that horrible taste

13) *The anise seeds lodged in the teeth of the corpse*

14) The opal ink scrolling the single page of her skin

 *In the High Country*

In the High Country

Some days I am happy to be no one
The shifting grasses

In the May winds are miraculous enough
As they ripple through the meadow of lupine

The field as iridescent as a Renaissance heaven
& do you see that boy with his arms raised

Like one of Raphael's angels held within
This hush & this pause & the sky's lapis expanse?

That boy is my son & I am his only father
Even when I am no one

The Future

There's a nightingale asleep in my palm
My friends tell me repeatedly
& some of them with great tenderness
My nightingale is certainly dead

Yet when she lifts & flies away
They recoil in horror
You've misunderstood I tell them all
As I hold out my open hand

You see? That line you fear is nothing
Simply an ordinary childhood scar

From a Bridge

I saw my mother standing there below me
On the narrow bank just looking out over the river

Looking at something just beyond the taut middle rope
Of the braided swirling currents

Then she looked up quite suddenly to the far bank
Where the densely twined limbs of the cypress

Twisted violently toward the storm-struck sky
There are some things we know before we know

Also some things we wish we would not ever know
Even if as children we already knew   & so

Standing above her on that bridge that shuddered
Each time the river ripped at its wooden pilings

I knew I could never even fate willing ever
Get to her in time

Waiting

This had all happened while I was waiting
Though I know I should have seen it coming after all

I knew she was your friend just
Perhaps a better friend than perhaps I'd first imagined

In any case I suppose it doesn't matter now
Neither the gunshot nor the vintage alligator suitcase

Nor the letter left on the dresser in her bedroom
Just off the hallway where I think I explained to you

I just happened to be waiting

Without Mercy, the Rains Continued

There had been
A microphone hidden

Beneath the bed
Of course I didn't realize it

At the time & in fact
Didn't know for years

Until one day a standard
Khaki book mailer

Arrived & within it
An old

Stained cassette tape
Simply labeled in black marker

"Him / Me / September 1975"
& as I listened I knew something

Had been asked of me
Across the years & loneliness

To which I simply responded
With the same barely audible

Silence that I had chosen then

Hungry Ghost

When I came to see you
It hurt me how thin you had become

In the months of addiction & disease
& although your particular abyss

Was a man & not a drug
The degradation was the same

The same wasting of the flesh
The same tapped-out well emptied

Of the least leaf of emotion
The same frozen rage

When I came to your hotel room
You were sitting in a hard chair

Just by the window
Half-slumped & distracted

Looking out at the persistent rain
Then silently back at me

Your ghost your own ghost
Had already come

She sat by you at the small table
& she was so hungry

At one point she reached over
Reached right inside you

& slowly twisted off a moist
Wafer of your heart

She put it in her mouth
& let it sit a moment on her tongue

Her lips parting in a way both
Petulant & suggestive

It was clear she would eat
All of you

I walked into the bathroom
& at the dulled zinc sink

I rinsed one by one
The fat spring strawberries

I'd brought you from the ranch
I put them in the white

Ceramic bowl
I'd carried from our kitchen

& without a word simply placed it
On the table

Just beside your ghost
She stared at me & then only

At the fleshy rubies awaiting her
& ate until only a few

Rivulets of blood traced
The bottom of the bowl & the green

Crowns she'd torn from
Their bodies

Lay scattered where
They had fallen at her feet

At last she seemed sated
Placated or even bored

She barely looked over as
I wrapped you in your overcoat

You glanced at her
& she at you

The rain
Still steady at the pane

& then I realized you could
Not stand

Alone & so I lifted you up
To take you home

In the Mojave

Then one of the bikers
Went at the other — a quick

Steel flash & a breathless
Grunt made it clear

He'd taken the brunt
Of the blade in his gut

As a low quiver then
A scream stalled on the lips

Of a girl about sixteen
Sitting at their table

& the woman by her
Was barely able

To hustle her outside
Before the whole place exploded—

Bottles smashing, shots . . .
Then it was over

& sprawled at my feet
One of the bikers dead

& the neat bone handle
Stood in the clot

Of blood barely seeping
From the black leather

Of this shadow twin my
Once now fallen brother

for Thom Gunn

Human Fields

It was she thought
A glorious trail coiling

Through the jungle beneath
The terraces & pancake layers

Of viridian leaves & limbs as
The parrots & howler monkeys

Delivered the day's editorial
Although she knew

She was hiking along those
Clearings & fields

Where hundreds of bodies
Had been shoveled into shelves

Of earth & sockets of rock
Villages hacked entirely to pieces

& planted haphazardly in the ruts
& furrows & she made herself recall

These were now human fields
No longer given over to local crops

From which at times a stray
Stalk of mud-caked shinbone

Or some misguided white rake of
A hand might reach up

Out of its bed as if
A new order had been announced

As if some heaven of actual memory
Had begun to radiate at last beyond

The cold & actual sky

My Friend Says

When my friend says he's
Walking closer to sadness
I know he means his own
Yet I also know precisely

What he means & he means
The gods he once admired
Because for so long they
Seemed to admire him

Have emptied their quivers
Into his flesh his very flesh
& he says this to me
Because he knows I too stood

In this exact moonlight
Stripped of every possibility
& divine protection
Except for a silver medallion

Of St. Sebastian hanging
Like a noose around my neck
& if the night that night was
A mirror then I believe so too

Was I the plain reflection
Of the long sadness of my friend

Cambria Pines

She'd answered her phone
In the dream & still
He was not there
Though earlier that night

He'd been reading
Her letters every single letter
Written on 12 × 15 papers she'd
Collaged with pieces of perhaps

Wallpaper postcards magazines
& a few shots of her wedding
Where she'd danced with her elegant
Handsome father & one taken

Not long after the birth of her
Son who in the photograph
She's hoisting onto her shoulder
Both infant & mother naked

In a stand of Cambria pines
A humid forest of primeval need
Their futures their bodies held
For this moment ecstatic & whole

Harvest

She thought of the wheat
Flaked with gold freckles

& the dark combine raking
The fields with its blades

As she stood in the harness
Of black leather & silver studs

Her nipples firm in the cold
Basement chamber

& as she imagined the dray horse
Foamy with the sweat of its labors

She saw the whip that she held
Flail once again against his withers

The Fixer

Perhaps it's not as you
First imagined

My specialty is people
Those beyond hope

& the details of recovery
They are the ones I will redeem

With my death or my love
Whichever seems more

Expedient at the time
I am a storm of electrons

Some devilish sleight of hand
In the heavens

A swelling consolation ravishing
The landscape of clouds

Blinding everyone if only
For an instant to

The carefully determined
Sorrow of their lives

Creque Alley

For sixteen years or more
She said she'd slept only

With black men either African
Or Caribbean she'd picked up

In the reggae & zouk bars
In Creque Alley during her time

In San Francisco doing phone
Solicitation by day & sex trade

By night her blonde hair by then
In exquisite cornrows down to

The middle of her back &
To break the cycle she admitted

Was killing her decided to
Marry one for the money & so

The green card he required
& another after he'd chained her

To the bed & kept her for weeks
Before she'd agreed & no

She didn't know where either of
Her husbands might be though

She now lived spitting distance
Of Point Lobos where one day

She'd stood far out on the rocks
As the tide came in & called me

On her cell saying listen to the surf
In which I am about to die

& I said No you're far too sick to die
& then she laughed & said please

Don't ever write about my illness
Which I despise though say

Anything you want about my father
Fucking me again & again

But please nothing of the way the virus
Has melted my body to bone

Then your horrible friends will know
All of my life before you & diagnosis

I will claim again now as my own

The Peaks

Some mornings it's hard
To ignore the chill

Of the nearby peaks
Though the day promises

To be warm once
The sun fully sweeps this

Narrow alpine valley
Where her body lies

Leaving the Valley

It was nothing really
Just the red moon

Above the stairway or
Maybe the old man

In his faded black suit
Tipping back the thin milky

Bottle beneath the stars
It was nothing really

To get worked up about
The way she stepped out

Onto the landing the door
To her room left

Slightly ajar its
Scarlet bulb a single blood pearl

She'd lost
In the blackened dark

It was really nothing
Or maybe it was just the way

She pointed her white boot
Or the way

The cat swept in
From the damp air or how

She'd turn silently to you
As the whole weight

Of the night fell
Or maybe it was really nothing

To you or to her or
Maybe it was simply she began

To hate the way you'd run
Your index finger

The length of the seam
On her stockings or maybe it was

Nothing really nothing
Like that at all just

That she despised the way
You looked distractedly away

As the waiter stood there waiting
& I suppose it doesn't matter now

How you missed that single low
Step up from the curb

One night & fell stumbling
To your knees before her

How you stayed that way almost
It seemed forever until

There was nothing really no really
Nothing left for you

To beg her for
Really nothing left no

Nothing left for you to beg
Her for at all

In memory of R. B. Kitaj

Reckless Wing

The window was open & a horse ran
Along the far edge of our field

You sat just opposite me
At our small kitchen table

& with one unbroken gesture
Swept your arm across its yellow

Formica clearing onto the floor
Coffee cups plates thatched with rinds

Of toast scarred by yolk newspapers
Notebooks & all of those distances

That'd gathered for months settling
Over everything & across this expanse

You raised your eyes to mine to make
Plain another new beginning

Piñon

She lit the piñon incense
She'd brought from the pueblo

& stood naked in the lantern's
Cream light before slipping

Over her shoulders
The black wool ceremonial sheath

Of the corn dance so I could see
If only for that one evening

The true name she'd given
The ancient body of her sacrifice

The Girl Who Lived in the Rain

The girl who lived in the rain

Came down from her cabin
Up on the mountain at that Y

Where the two creeks joined

& flowed into the valley
Alongside her small village & by

A metal shed where her father lived

With his pine carvings of geese
& crows that he worked at

Every day even the day

His daughter married & moved
To her husband's raw homestead

Of salvaged planks & plastic

Built high in the fog shadows
Of perpetual rain & when

She came along the street toward

Her father's workshop those who
Looked up saw she seemed to be

Wearing a woven black cloud

Circling her loose & bloody hair
Sudden sprigs of lightning

Forking out from her skull

& those who looked saw the rain
On her brow & cheeks & her lips

Saw all of the rain falling nowhere

Except within the vortex of her
Own body until a man's blood also

Washed from her hands

The Boy

The boy in the sunflowers
Hates the swirling crows

As he walks the narrow rows
Below reading aloud the Sunday

Scripture he must recite to the whole
Of the congregation

& the crows' arch commentaries
& complaints punctuate

Each elegant passage from Paul
The boy may hate the crows

But one in particular it seems
Certainly admires him circling

As it does lower & lower until
The boy believes it might

Actually land on his shoulder
The way the enormous black parody

Of an angel spreads its wings
& hangs momentarily

Almost directly before his face
& the boy knows he believes

He has seen his own shadow
The boy knows he has seen beyond

What boys are allowed to see
& if the crow insists that he acknowledge

The dark then the boy right there
In the waving cathedral of

Sunflowers simply lets himself
Fall to his knees

Flooded by the light both black
& golden around him

As the pulse of the river hymn
Begins just at the far boundary of the field

& then he too begins to sing

Quicksilver Girl *(Mt. Tamalpais, 1967)*

Safe inside my old Skylark
We settle against the thick seats
To watch the rain lay trails down
The dust & blow waterfalls

Of smoke through the cracked
Panes of the side windows
As she tells me once again how
She'd run away from Fresno

To live with Quicksilver that year
Deep within serpent-licked roads
& acid redwoods until she was
Busted & brought back with her

Hair shaved to a boy's bristle
Blue wrists shivering in handcuffs
She says it every time just like
A low note on a tin saxophone

Held & buzzing in the broken speaker
Of the car radio driving again
Somewhere you can almost remember
A sad solo she turns on going nowhere

for Gillis

Paisley *(Haight-Ashbury, 1967)*

There is a rope leading
From the present tense
To the hand of a mysterious
Woman who is excessively

Thin & cloaked in a cape
Gray as shadow
Beneath which her nude body
Is tattooed with delicate

Intricately detailed
Floridly inked paisleys each
A plump comma or swelling
Inverted question mark

Along her skin the raw beige
Of blank parchment
Yet the hillsides are so lustrous
Today is the beautiful season

The leaves glint with fresh
Emerald enamels & the tulips
& the iris & the yellow narcissus
Lift up their luscious heads

Out of the past tense & these open
Hands of a mysterious woman

The Empty Frame

In the late spring or early
Summer of the year my family

Would drive past these fields
As we'd make our way in a black

Dodge up Tollhouse Road for
Shaver Lake or Huntington Lake—

Places my father often told me
He'd spent the best bar none

Summers of his life—yet in my
Own teens it was instead to these

Same foothills of the Sierras
I'd return always these meadows

Of long stiff marsh grass gone
Dry in the heat randomly stitched

By the spring wildflowers
& slow needles of piercing sunlight

I'd walk alone in those low hills
Or with the girl

I'd soon marry very soon to be also
The mother of our son

I need to tell you this now
Because I have you by me the one

I've waited for to sketch finally
The story of a boy who'd lie

At night in those fields believing
A world beyond always awaited

Restless in its insistent music
Now after the years of sickness

& lies I'm asking you in your
Stillness to hold this ledger of

Spring accounts & recall the plain
Mariposa lilies & the goldenrod

& the crowns of thistle & the yellow
Star-tulips & the clusters of wild clover

Dusted white & the faint musk mallow
& the endless waves of lupine

All blooming in a way I thought
Might hold me safely forever

& I need to tell you sometimes
I'd fall asleep out in those open fields

Always near the abandoned farm
I loved—its shaky one-room cottage

Still standing though by then releasing
Its boards to the steady seasons

Its crippled barn already long broken
To its knees & rotting & holy & yet

Wherever in the world I'd travel
It was the memory of that cottage

I'd carry with me I'm not sure why
Even so derelict & so many years

Abandoned it felt always somehow
Like home to me & last night at dusk

I drove again after these forty years out
Tollhouse Road along the long stretch

Leading past Academy & the cemetery
Where Ollie's family still presides

Then I pulled over at the familiar dirt
& gravel turnout where the same

Weathered planks & fence posts
Rose cracked & swiped by long grasses

Below the white limbs of that ancient oak
I walked out into the meadow

Leading to the old farm & though I saw
The cottage itself was finally gone

& only odd uneven squares of cracked
Foundation blocks still stood

Sinking into the long white grass
I could also see   I swear to you just

Above & slightly to the right of the three
Concrete steps leading up to what

Now was nothing & no doorway
I could see hanging there impossibly

In the air exactly as it had always hung
Yet now only as the empty frame

Of the landscape nailed upon
The crossbeam of the blackening night

The same kitchen window that once
Opened onto these fields of wildflowers

& it floated precisely where it had
As if the cottage itself were yet standing

As if it were now my own window
& I could see that a light was burning

Once again within as if yes you were
Somehow waiting exactly

As I'd imagined these past months
Waiting at the burled black oak

Table with warped legs & its surface
Scarred by your bracelets & keys

Having your evening coffee over
A field guide of trails or alpine blossoms

& so I need now to ask you
Which of the old journals did you first

Open to a map of my long wandering
When did you first know I'd come back

& how did you find yourself here
& how did you know this single lantern

You are reading by was the last possible
Light to lead me home?

Late Offerings

Beyond the dark
Late offerings

& the immortality of
Sleep within

A light bestowed
Reflected along

The cheekbones of a face
Paling beyond

The black orbits
& final hymns

The dirge of a lone
Piper at the prow

Of the night barge
Beyond any formal

Essence of departure
Release me to

The presence
Of the present

Its difficult passage
Its steep ascent

The shale-splintered
Cirrus-scaled aperture of

Phantasmagoric sky

The Auroras

The Auroras

I. DAWN AURORA

The nothing you know is as immaculate a knowing
as any moment moving from a distance into dawn.
All of the awakenings, or the old unconscious lies . . .
I'd waited all night, holed up in Selene's derelict houseboat—
drinking tea, drinking scotch, thinking of the rain
that night in Camden Town when she went missing for hours,
coming back only to say, Sayonara baby; thinking of
the way so many things touch their own fates. The motorcycle

heads for the cliff, or the bus stops just before the bench.
Everything seems more shabby in the dusk; everything glorious
holds its light. Look to your sons, look to your daughters.
Look to the blades rising out of the dark lawn. Don't worry;
each of your myths remains emblazoned upon the air. The way
the wind moves across the vellum of the mountain,
as the silence lifts its chords from the old piano. In the still dark
& still uncertain dawn, there begins that slow revelation larger

than the mind's, as the light grows coronal, & the house fills
with those elaborate agendas of the day. The monastery & philosophy—
this morning, both seem so far away.

II. LAGO DI COMO

The blood of the visible hangs like blossoms of bougainvillea
as they turn & twist along the lattice of limbs shading your
terrace, stretching like a ruby squid across one corner of the stone
villa above the lake. We sit looking out over the unqualified excellence
of the morning, & there is nothing you might desire to recall. You
believe in a space that is as large as logic, that is as logical as the word.

Tell me. What is the "beautiful," what is the "lost," & what lives still, just
at the edge of the sound of the trees? It could be the syllables of habit;
it could be a single phrase of gratitude . . . or an unbroken prayer. Tell me.
What will stay, & what will hold its grace & lasting ease?

III. AUTUMN AURORA

The illusionist steps to the stage. Everything
he claims will be, will be. I know because I've watched him
before the curtains began to part, & I've seen he is not just
one man, but he is also a woman. He is as multiple
as the rain. He is all children in the future—those children
both the woman & the man he is will bring from their couplings,
their embraces, & those silences of the clasped plural of their

nights, their individual nights. How have you left me? You have
left me with my hopes. How have you dreamed of me? You
have dreamed of me beneath the cool of the evening. There I am,
holding my dulcimer, holding my mandolin. There I am, singing
to you, always, singing to you, always, across the blade of time.
In the monograph of dawn, all of the tendencies of shifting light . . .
& now the bells are sounding. This evening, we will discover

only the fragrance of the October moon.

IV. FLORENTINE AURORA

I saw what would proclaim itself as *beauty-beyond-surface*.
It was the rarest of days. I'd walked directly from the train station
& found the gallery empty, yet filled with a golden light as if dozens of
gilt bees rose lazily to the eaves, each a reflected particle of the afternoon.
It was a whole universe lifted by the painting; it was a universe
    that mirrored
the afternoon—& its singular burnishing within the painting—
    & the young
women, articulating the angles of desire, the hopeless erotic fortune
that proves itself in beauty. The shell of the day unfolding, the perfume of
the moment filling every pore we call the imagination. The day,
    today, seems
inexhaustible. This is my praise; this is my proclamation. This is
    the apple
I place on the white plate, before you. This is my metaphysics
    of possibility.
This is the fury of the present. This is the memory of the questions
I offer like pewter goblets. Let us share what remains, while it remains.

V. THE AURORA CALLED DESTINY

Selene was hearing voices again. It had become something
she was apt to do now & then; she heard the voices,
but she could not recall the names. . . . When she slept, voices
choired her into the heavens, & when she awoke they lay her
along the bed of dawn. She was precise & independent
in this illumination, & she found herself in the descent of many wings,

like a vortex of angelic understandings. Everything that seemed to sing
echoed in harmony around her, & the fevered happiness broke
like sweat along her skin. If the body shows it is the soft
white of wax, if the fox moves across the field & the white meadows
by the black woods, then what do we know of our deaths? What do we
know of the impossible weathers we must transcend?

                    What do we know of the milk
of the future & the milk of the end? Here is your destiny—it is the color
of lapis & mirrors, of the glass which empties itself of time, of every
whisper. Here, at the oak dining table, place your palms upward facing, so
the sky can read the lines crossing there, & the grain of what remains.
This is not the epitaph you imagine. This is not some phantom

fear. Or else, I suppose, it is.

VI. THE SWAN

Nakedness only is never marriage, just as the pilgrim
looks beyond all fictive weavings of our oracles. In my notebook,
I keep my list of questions ready for the stranger at the crossroads:
How can I keep my life luminous, & how can I keep the day delivered?
Where does my constant taste for evasion end & the altar begin?
Where does the word become the Word, & why does the flesh
    remain flesh?

In the quiet of the park, the water spreads out before us, & the single
swan cuts across the water's blackness like a piece of music, like the fall
of an iris upon the table at dawn. Where have the minstrels gone, where
the loves that were lifted up in fables like the mantles of sorcerers
& the manes of their stallions, that white, white hair? I believe
    the blank wall

remains blank for several lifetimes, & then finally there is the inked reason
of the figure. Look, the stranger's nails are lacquered silver, as she stands
at the roadside, white as light. There, with a feather boa & auras
    of the notice
we allow to be born of sexual repose, with the movement that becomes
    the very
fragrance of the vines, & all pulses of afterward, & all the drowsy
refractions of her fatal, far-wingèd independence.

VII. GHOST AURORA

All of the apostles, the fortune-tellers, all of those committed
to the origins of reason or faith—each is now lost in the hum

of her or his own deepening meditation. What could be the purpose
of those songs the troubadour from Avignon brought us in his
    leather bag?

What could be the meaning of the carvings of green falcons along
the gourd-like back of his lute? What could be more useful than a loving

principle lifted slowly out of particles, like the frond of a morning fern
uncurling? Take up your coat; take up the morning. This is what it means

to lure the phantom out of the dark, until she lifts us into the space
    of song.

VIII. AURORE PARISIENNE

Selene became the pilot of her fate, dressed in careless breezes
& summer birds. Her sandals were stitched with fire & the summer moths
hovered at her toes. She shuffled in the chaos & she could not help,
    she said,
but drink the poison of her past, every mortal coil, every green core. All

those ancient probabilities echoed as she spoke, each in its own
    pastoral refrain,
like light lifted from a sepulcher, like the oblivion of the lamp & its
    cold globe
standing for the illumined but lost spirit. There, the abyss & the storm
& her desire all came to be one. If the forest beyond arose, it was
    the forest she
understood. Who else could move this way, except one already lost . . . as
    she said,

Think of me walking along the Seine, as I think of you in the twilight
    & the echo
of the day, lifting very slowly two ancient books before you . . . their songs
    arising still
even in the automatic flak of traffic, even as the swallows & martins
    slowly swirl.

IX. PÈRE LACHAISE

The names that have been unnamed arise, cold & clear
as the inscriptions upon the virgin stone. There, the rubies shone
against the onyx; there, those charnel house weathers, & the love
that must emerge like love. On the other side of the world, my
best friend dressed only in small brass cymbals. They were the size
of quarters & linked by either wire or cord. He had no idea what it
meant. He knew only as he moved each movement was announced by
the most glorious sound, chimes & rattles & an iridescence in the ear—
the golden weather of himself shimmering everywhere. When they
found him later, dead, they said how pagan he'd become in his nakedness,

in his glory.

X. THE BOOK

What is it about the motives of the night? All of those lovers
walking in the luster of their pasts. The strings of melody plucked
in the lightness of sleep.
                    What is it about the body
awakening beside you, rippling with that ultimate, jubilant fire?

Here in the strange, strange inn at the edge of the wood
there is the sacrifice of the leaves, all of the vestments abandoned.
All of the false stitching of the heraldry hanging, those banners of
death along the walls. I could not tell you, but there, outside,
the hinds hid & the hounds hung their heads, & it was in the room

above the inn, the raucous calamity of the inn, there by the bed,

she stood naked, clothed only in the knowledge of herself,
knowing the spider hanging in the corner between the raw beams
& the armoire was something as unofficial as the end—& there,
naked, redolent with the flames of the fire, with those embers rendering
light like language . . . she was, herself, a moving myth, self-announced

as any emblem of a life unfolding upon the air, the light, though the book
that she opened, the only book she knew, remained flat as a world,
    its pages

made luminous by the mind.

XI. THE AURORA OF THE MIDNIGHT INK

Will you really walk from one edge of the city to the other
dressed only in illusion & shame? How can I urge you to turn back?
Selene, when we return, we return to the book. The book opens,
& the world unfolds into its latticework of hymns. It is the excruciating
alchemy by which the spirit lives. I will live there with you, in the hotel
of the spirit, where the sheets are changed daily. Every instinct for

darkness is countered by yet another instinct for the light. Stand with me,

as I stand beside you in my jacket from Verona, its deep slate blue of
the gentlemen on their passeggiata. Here, take my pen, the scarred
    Montblanc
or the old Parker 50—it's your choice tonight—& write to me
in the script of the present, write to me about those long white petals of a
carpenter's shavings uncurling from his plane; write to me & tell me how
the mind can require such certainty of the dark. Any unfolding is an

unfolding into light, that unlocked origami of the light—the light slowly
lining again those faces, those facets, of our yet unfolding story.

XII. DARK AURORA

What a beautiful letter you wrote to me. It was as ripe
as a planet, & as much to the point. It was filled I saw not
with revelations or expectations. It was a space that expanded
like space. All I could do was respond with the poor reflex of intellect,
which is to say the insufficiency of a hedgehog & the modest vocabulary
of a saint. Darkness, darkness. What unfolds folds out away from us.

If death has a form, it is the form of departure. If death has a form,
it is lit by darkness. Everything we've looked for all these years,
everything together we've called some necessity of invention, any
syllable & symbol, every penetrating & luminous or prodigious desire,
every carved line on every page has emptied into this flesh, this flash
of revelation, this form which is no memory, which is our dark, the form

of dark, & darkness in its final form.

About the Author

Over the course of his career, David St. John has been honored with many of the most significant prizes for poets, including fellowships from the National Endowment for the Arts and the John Simon Guggenheim Memorial Foundation, the Rome Fellowship, an Award in Literature from the American Academy and Institute of Arts and Letters, a grant from the Ingram Merrill Foundation, as well as the O. B. Hardison Prize, a career award from the Folger Shakespeare Library for teaching and poetic achievement.

David St. John is the author of ten collections of poetry, including *Study for the World's Body*, nominated for the National Book Award in Poetry, as well as a volume of essays, interviews, and reviews titled *Where the Angels Come Toward Us*. He is also the co-editor, with Cole Swensen, of *American Hybrid: A Norton Anthology of New Poetry*. He teaches in the PhD program in literature and creative writing at the University of Southern California, and lives in Venice Beach.